OVER THE SUMMER WATER

OVER THE SUMMER WATER

ELIZABETH MCFARLAND

PREFACE BY DANIEL HOFFMAN

ORCHISES
WASHINGTON
2008

Library of Congress Cataloging in Publication Data

McFarland, Elizabeth, 1922-2005.
    Over the summer water / Elizabeth McFarland ; preface by
    Daniel Hoffman.
      p. cm.
    Poems.
    ISBN 978-1-932535-15-0 (alk. paper)
    I. Title.
    PS3613.C439O84 2008
    811'.6—dc22

                        2007022514

ACKNOWLEDGMENTS

Thanks to the editors of the following magazines in which some of these poems first appeared: *Crossroads:* "Reminders" (2007); *Florida Magazine of Verse:* "Myself" (1941); *Hudson Review:* "Lost Gold," "Love's Touch," "Off Little Deer Isle" (2007); *Ladies Home Journal:* "A Little Liking," "Communication," "Elegy for Donald McFarland," "If I Could Breathe," "His Lashes" [titled "The Young One"], "Mother," "No Other Love," "Over the Summer Water," "Plums," "Speech" and "Two Voices" (1950-1958); *Poetry:* "Exiles" (1947), "I Thought of Donne" and "The Rejection" (2007); *Scholastic Magazine:* "Penates" (1946); *Sewanee Review:* "Climbers," "Feed My Birds," "Lost Girl" (2007).

Daniel Hoffman's preface was first published in *Crossroads* (2007).

Cover Painting: *Pond Island* by Peter Diemond.

Manufactured in the United States of America

Orchises Press
P. O. Box 320533
Alexandria
Virginia
22320-4533

G6E4C2A

CONTENTS

A POET WHO BROUGHT POETRY
TO THE MILLIONS

Elizabeth McFarland was such a modest, private person, she would have been astonished had she known she'd be featured in *The New York Times Magazine* on Christmas Sunday as one of the most notable persons who died in 2005. She is the only editor in the history of publishing in America who brought into six million households new work of the most eminent poets—W. H. Auden, Marianne Moore, Richard Eberhart, Mark Van Doren, John Ciardi, Theodore Roethke, Walter De la Mare—and the then most promising younger ones, among them Maxine Kumin, Sylvia Plath, Adrienne Rich, Donald Hall, Galway Kinnell, William Jay Smith, William Stafford, and John Updike. This is a service to literary culture not likely to be repeated. From 1948 to 1961 she was poetry editor of *The Ladies' Home Journal,* where she also published her own romantic, lyrical poems. As the 1960s began, the Curtis Publishing Company's manager retired; his replacements made timid, money-losing decisions that led to the loss of the *LHJ* editors-in-chief. No wide-circulation magazine since has published poems as did the *LHJ* when Elizabeth McFarland, with the assent of her editor-in-chief, Bruce Gould, influenced the taste of millions of readers and brought leading poets the most generous payments they ever received for their poems.

That this was possible reflected the role of magazines in encouraging, after the Civil War, the role of women as the keepers of culture. In the newly industrial, mercantile and capitalist nation, men hustled in the business world to support their families and make the country grow. Their wives would comprise a leisure class, pursuing artistry in quilting, knitting, and home decoration, and the fine arts in painting, and reading and writing fiction and poetry. So it was, before the 1960s, that journals such as *Vanity Fair*, *Harper's Bazaar*, and *Mademoiselle* published fiction by leading authors. In presenting poetry, however, the *Journal*, with six to ten poems each month, was paramount. Bruce Gould and his wife Beatrice wanted their magazine to uplift as well as entertain their readers (in addition, of course, to providing them with household, marital, and medical advice), but the verse they published was mediocre until Elizabeth McFarland was brought onto the staff.

Poetry was central to her life. At six years old she was the darling of the Harrisburg Manuscript Club, brought there by her great-aunts to recite her rhymes. As a schoolgirl, Liz crammed her memory with anthologies of poems, and was writing her own. When she was nine, her parents were divorced; a few years later her father was remarried to a Southern woman of strict decorum, and took his four children—Liz was the eldest—to his wife's home in South Jacksonville, at Glenlea, the estate beside the St. Johns River where the composer Frederick Delius had lived. Liz won the nation-wide high school poetry contest of *Scholastic Magazine*, placed second in fiction, was graduated from the Bartram School, and was offered a tuition scholarship to Vassar. This, however, her stepmother said she couldn't accept, for with three younger children to educate the family couldn't send Liz north. Florida State College for Women was then a good liberal arts school where, guided by inspiring literature and journalism professors, reading the same poems I did at Columbia, she won the poetry prizes and edited the literary magazine. Then she came to New York City, to find her way in the literary world.

In August 1946, I was just out of the Army Air Force, resuming my junior year. On a sultry night I walked out of my stifling dorm room, down Broadway for 18 blocks to the Thalia, an art theatre showing a different film classic each night. Its lobby, like those in London or Paris, had a coffee bar and paintings on the walls. Arriving between shows, I noticed in the queue a pair of young women. One really caught my attention; she seemed, even across the room, so vibrant and attractive. I managed to join their dialogue, and when the bill changed, sat next to the one I favored. After the film I took them to a bar nearby on Broadway. We sounded each other out—what brought you to New York? Saying "summer school" would sound rather square, so, quickly changing the subject, I said I'd had a stroke of luck that afternoon, finding, in the Strand Bookstore, a copy of Oscar Williams's anthology, *New Poems 1944*. I already owned *New Poems 1940*. Wishing to appear *really* avant-garde, I added, "I suppose you're familiar with these collections?"

Oh, she replied, she had *New Poems 1942* and *1943*—there was none in '41. In a city teeming with eligible young women, by the smiling of what gods was I permitted to pick up the poetry editor of *Scholastic Magazine!* There began the intermingling of our books, and of our lives. Our marriage seemed foreordained, and lasted 57 years.

On *Scholastic* Liz conducted a Round Table, corresponding with talented high school poets, printing the best of their verses. Also, under various *noms de plume*, she filled in for other staffers with articles on teen topics, and, as "Valkyrie Weed," contributed short fiction. The magazine was deluged with entries in the national contests Liz when a student had won; now she had to screen the poems, stories, and also essays. English teachers as well as their students loved the magazine, in part because Liz interviewed such real poets as Marianne Moore and José Garcia Villa. When his first book, *Have Come, Am Here* appeared in 1942, Villa was widely hailed in the absence of other poets away in the war. He was from the Philippines, and introduced his country to modernism—Eliot, Cummings, Edith Sitwell. His next book, portentously titled *Volume Two*, was a sensation too, as the only book of poems ever published with a comma between every word. This,worked,rather, well,in,his,poem,about,a,centipede, but elsewhere seemed rather an affectation, like writing backwards on the flyleaf so his inscriptions had to be held to a mirror to be read.

When Liz wrote to Marianne Moore, c/o her publisher, asking for an interview, she was soon invited to come to Brooklyn. In her excitement at actually meeting the poet she so admired, Liz forgot to bring the copies of *What are Years* and *Nevertheless* she hoped Miss Moore would sign. The next day she enclosed her thank-you note for the interview and tea in an envelope containing the books. Two days later the books arrived from 260 Cumberland Street in a re-used publishers' carton, wrapped in a page from *The New York Sun*, and inscribed "For Elizabeth McFarland with affectionate good wishes / Marianne Moore / March 3, 1948." Inside the cover of *Nevertheless*, Miss Moore enclosed two booklets from the post office of 24 three-cent stamps (then the cost of a posting a letter), plus two loose stamps, scrupulously totaling $1.50, exactly the price of the little volume. On one of the booklets she had written, in her spidery hand, "In lieu of purchase—I'd like to have given you the book."

That was the last interview Liz wrote for *Scholastic*; a few weeks later she was hired by the *LHJ* and moved to Philadelphia. After Liz died I attended a reading by Rhina Espaillat. Looking through her most recent book, I was startled to notice, among the acknowledgments, *Ladies' Home Journal*—which had not, to my knowledge, published a poem since 1961. I asked when her poem had appeared there. "Oh, that was in 1948," she said. I replied it must have been accepted by my late wife. "Elizabeth McFarland!" she exclaimed, 57 years later remembering the name of the editor whose encouragement launched her career. She'd been a 16-year old high school junior whose teacher had sent her poem to the *Journal* without telling her. Liz's letter was the first of several giving the girl confidence that she really could write poems, and confirming her desire to do so.

Rhina must have been paid a dollar per line. At this time *Poetry* paid 50¢, *The New Yorker* two dollars. Learning how much authors of articles received for their prose, Liz proposed that poetry was underpaid in the *Journal*, and, to attract better poets, she persuaded Mr. Gould to raise the fee to $2, and before long to $10. She wrote to poets she knew and to others whose work she hoped would be submitted, and soon the roster in the contents page contained names well-known then and today. This generosity was much appreciated. Bill Stafford wrote that she had helped him meet his mortgage payments, John Ciardi that he could now winter-proof his house in Metuchen. Philip Booth thanked her for a much-needed augmenting of his writing fellowship. Liz had become a one-woman Guggenheim Foundation.

On her job about a year, Liz thought wouldn't it be a *coup* to publish a poem by W. H. Auden. We didn't yet know him, in fact had seen him only once, in the Spring of '47, when, fooling no one, I smuggled Liz in her trench coat, trousers, and her hair done up in a beret, into a meeting of the all-male Boar's Head Poetry Society (Columbia wouldn't go co-ed for nearly forty years) to hear the great one read his poems. Now, in 1950, responding to her request he sent a 26-line poem, "Secrets," quickly accepted and published in the August issue. The correspondence about this has disappeared so I don't know what Auden was paid, but it was surely more than the ten dollars lesser lights received. In 1952 I invited Auden to read for the Philadelphia Art Alliance, and, at the dinner before the program, Liz asked would he send another poem to the *LHJ*? In his note thanking me for "taking care" of him he included a poem, "Fleet Visit." My guess is that he stuffed into that envelope the latest poem he had written; it described, in a couple of stanzas, innocent middle-class boys on shore leave, but told that they got "drunk" and were approached by "a whore." This obviously wouldn't do for the *Journal*. My files reveal this much, but not who declined the poem. It must have been I, since he had sent it not to Liz but to me asking that I pass it on to her. Auden held no grudge when, the following year, he chose my ms. for the Yale Series of Younger Poets. Liz used to say she lived in fear of having to send a rejection note to W. H. Auden, so it's obvious she hadn't done so with this one, nor, since he didn't try the *LHJ* again, did she ever need to return a poem of his.

By 1957 I was teaching at Swarthmore College and invited Richard Eberhart to give a reading. Ever confident of his role as a bard since he wrote in fits of "extreme intuition," Dick was nonetheless insecure about each new poem. He sent me several, asking my opinion. Of course Liz read them too, and found one she really liked. She telegraphed that she'd want to submit it to the *Journal* where, if accepted, he'd be paid $10 a line. Dick had already sent the poem to *Botteghe Oscura*, but its editor, Princess Caetani, acceded to his request to release it. The poem was a fresh, closely observed New England cadenza on the theme of Wordsworth's "Resolution and Independence." Swiftly accepted, "The Clam Diggers and Diggers of Sea Worms" brought Dick Eberhart a hefty check for its 46 lines. He wrote to thank Liz for what would "pay this summer's rent in Maine." He must have boasted of his good fortune in the Dartmouth Faculty Club, for in the next few weeks Liz was deluged by poems, verses, limericks, and jingles, none publishable, from just about every member of that college's English department.

The Goulds in the 1950s were supporters of the Academy of American Poets, and, having purchased tickets at $500 per place for its annual fund-raising, prize-giving dinner, gave them to Liz. Thus it was that when a photo was taken there of Marianne Moore wearing a triple orchid corsage, she stood between Liz in an off-the-shoulder white evening gown and me in black tie. Miss Moore was relieved to find Liz, someone she actually knew, among the donors. The photo appeared in the *New York Times Magazine* on Christmas Sunday, 2005. We saw Marianne Moore on another occasion, the Phi Beta Kappa initiation at Columbia in 1956. I don't recall who was the orator—probably Jacques Barzun—but we were there to hear Miss Moore read her poem, "Blessed is the Man." As soon as the ceremony ended Liz rushed up to Miss Moore and asked could she have the new poem for the *Ladies' Home Journal?* Miss Moore agreed, but Liz had overstepped her own role: she could choose and recommend poems, but their final acceptance required Bruce Gould's agreement. To encourage that assent, Liz sent him a telegram—"IF WE MOVE FAST WE CAN OUTBID MCCALLS FOR NEW POEM BY MARIANNE MOORE."

Mr. Gould of course saw through Liz's stratagem— *McCall's Magazine* didn't even publish poetry—but to bring out a new poem by Marianne Moore, then at the peak of her fame, appealed to him. There ensued a correspondence between Miss Moore and Miss McFarland, the poet insisting that *The Ladies' Home Journal* publish not only her poem but the notes in which her Puritan conscience acknowledged each of the sources of phrases she had borrowed—"Psalm 1:1," "Campaign manager's attack on the Eisenhower administration," a review in the *Times,* etc. Liz had to persuade her that such modest honesty would only confuse readers of the *Journal* not accustomed to footnotes, but after all the notes would appear with the poem in her forthcoming book. And indeed they are in *Like a Bulwark,* where acknowledgment is made to Elizabeth McFarland as well as to *The Ladies' Home Journal.*

Marianne Moore was overwhelmed to receive a check for $362.50 for her 29-line poem. For her, the recompense was $12.50 per line; in 2005, the last year given on the internet inflation calculator, in purchasing power that check was equivalent to $2,500. In 1958, at Liz's urging, Miss Moore let the *LHJ* have her poem "Boston," later retitled "In the Public Garden." At 62 lines this one brought her $775, equivalent in 2005 dollars to $5,084.93. This, no doubt, was the most generous check she had received for a single poem. She showered Liz with photos and clippings about the Boston festival for which the poem had been commissioned. (Liz gave these and her letters to the Moore Collection of the Rosenbach Library and Museum in Philadelphia.)

About 1,000 submissions reached Elizabeth McFarland, on average, every week. These she read, scanning every one in her search for good poems by unknown poets as well as by recognized names—among the then-prominent poets she published were Katherine Garrison Chapin, Elizabeth Coatsworth, Robert P. Tristram Coffin, Jean Garrigue, Rolphe Humphries, Eve Merriam, May Sarton, Jesse Stuart, Edward Weismuller. When our children were infants and toddlers, Liz worked mainly at home, her secretary Rita coming out by train to Swarthmore with the week's poems in a strapped carton like those college students use to send home their laundry. Rita returned to the office in Philadelphia, her carton filled with the last week's poems and drafts of letters to be typed for those accepted. Liz went to the office one or two days to sign these. Some of the rejected submissions, if written to mourn a recently lost child or from a would-be poet with a serious illness, needed letters too; as a family magazine the *LHJ* had a heart. Liz was very accomplished at quickly identifying the 99% in the slush pile, returned with printed slips. The possibles-but-not-quite-purchased, like unsuitable poems by former contributors or other published poets, required diplomatic letters.

One day, while in the office on Independence Square, Liz was called on by half a dozen grim-visaged men in uniform. The American Legion had convened in Philadelphia, and these members demanded to see the poetry editor who had turned down a contribution by the wife of one of their number. They'd come to object, and to threaten. If she didn't agree to publish the patriotic verse of Mrs. Legionnaire, they would insist at the convention that all members' wives cancel subscriptions to such an unAmer-ican magazine.

During the McCarthy hysteria and the prominence of the John Birch Society this threat had to be taken seriously. Liz looked at the page again, scanning its hyperpatriotic ejaculations, then said that while its sentiments did credit to the writer, she couldn't publish this in a conservative American family magazine. *The Ladies' Home Journal,* she told them, represented core American values, and this statement, that neither rhymed nor scanned and had no stanzas but was written in lines of all different lengths, would, to the Journal's readers, look *foreign.* Taken aback, the legionnaires grumblingly headed for the elevator. Liz earned her keep that day, protecting the *LHJ* from thousands of cancellations.

Some time after Edna St. Vincent Millay died, her sister Norma came on a poem in her hand that didn't turn up in any of her books. Thinking to place this find before the millions who'd read it in the *LHJ,* she bypassed the poetry editor and sent it directly to the top of the masthead, Bruce Gould. Of course he shared his excitement with Liz, but it was short-lived, for she immediately recognized that Millay had hand-copied a poem from Robert Louis Stevenson's *A Child's Garden of Verses,* and so saved the *Journal* from becoming the jape of the cognoscenti.

Liz took a leave of absence from editing when I taught in France, and we and our children spent the year abroad. Mr. Gould had hired a woman to run the poetry section, but, dissatisfied, replaced her with another—no more adequate than the first. He wrote Liz, half-jokingly— "With you at the poetry helm we got good poetry. Without you we get nothing. So please come back, dear girl, forsaking your husband and children. We need you bad!" She did come back and continued to fulfill her mission. During a later sabbatical, in 1961-62 when we were in London, Mr. Gould had Liz listed as employed though unsalaried, because, he said, there were threats of war in Europe and, were she included as Curtis Publishing Company personnel, pressure could be brought on the

American Embassy to hasten her and her family's repatriation.

In the event, she never returned to the *LHJ*, for, in a circulation war with *McCall's*, *Life*, and *Look*, the new Curtis managers lost the *Journal's* preeminence and rejected sound advice from the Goulds, who resigned. Poetry was killed in the *Journal* forever. Fiction and homemaking articles brought in advertisers, products could be named in the prose, but poems sold nothing. The *LHJ* never again attained the six and a quarter million readership it had under the Goulds. The Sixties had begun, and along with the general distrust of authority came changes in women's roles: now women justifiably demanded equality with men, holding the same jobs for the same salaries. Women's magazines no longer appealed to their readers as a leisure class lifting the candle of culture, but as consumers, and, in magazines competing with the *LHJ*, as sexually desirous and desirable. The great shift in mores was under way. I was then at Swarthmore, and later at the University of Pennsylvania; there was no suitable employment for Liz in the Philadelphia area. She directed her creative instincts into writing further poems, raising our children, and emulating her famous great-uncle, J. Horace McFarland, who had helped establish the National Parks Service and the American Rose Society, by cultivating magnolias and roses and landscaping our meadow overlooking Penobscot Bay on Cape Rosier. Our alternative life of long summers amid the tranquility and rugged grandeur of the Maine coast refreshed us.

This young woman who attracted and published so many eminent poets was of course a poet herself. She had, when still in school, immersed herself in the mellifluous versing of the silver poets of the English Renaissance; in Emily Dickinson's mysterious compression and metaphoric power; in Donne's astonishing imagery that presented "two souls [as] one... Like gold to aery thinness beat"; and in Hopkins with his sensuous language and heart-wringing intensity. She had early developed a style quite her own. Here is a poem, titled "Myself," written when she was nineteen:

> I have stood so long in this place
> I have lost account of my face.
> I have stared so long at this tree
> I am grown blossomy.
>
> In my branches, words
> Bicker like birds.

The cross-stitching between the words linked by rhyme with those by alliteration—the two most significant words both alliterate and rhyme—intensifies these lines, proof of her intuitive command of technique. With swift economy they tell that the poet loses her sense of self in meditation as she is transformed to a flowering part of nature, and her language, too, is alive and winged. This is the first poem in this book. A dozen of its others first appeared in *The Ladies' Home Journal,* not out of place among those by the famous and soon-to-be-famous contributors mentioned above.

After Liz died I found a folder containing her verses—some 70 poems, many to, for, or about our children—these I hope are destined for a second volume. I have chosen and arranged the poems in the present book, since she had never done so. The temper of the times did not welcome her personal style. In the late 1940s and '50s, when most of her poems were written, there were two poetry movements dominating the *zeitgeist* and the literary magazines. One was the formal, metaphysical, ironic, impersonal style derived from the example and papal influence of T.S. Eliot. The other, in reaction to this, was the so-called confessional school, flat-lined free verse often in language indis-tinguishable from newspaper prose, recounting personal traumas—rebellion against a tyrannical parent, sexual abuse, alcoholism or drug addiction, the acrimonies of divorce, thoughts of suicide. Liz was attracted to neither of these period styles. Hers was a romantic imagination, in love with the sounds of the language and committed to intensifying feeling through indirection, subtleties and surprises of metaphor.

"Plums" treats a subject many contemporaries would offer in explicit, tabloid versions. Her resonant, sensuous language, precise observations, and the inference that engages the reader's imagination evoke and explore the emotion embodied in the poem. The feeling is the more intense for being implied. In "No Other Love" the passion summoned is lyrical and direct, in "Two Voices" poignant yet serious beneath its playful wit.

When in our thirties the idea of our own death is a distant abstraction, serving at most to stir imagination and evoke images. "Reminders" is both an homage to Emily Dickinson and, half a century before needed, an assuagement of the grief of the poet's survivor. Her title poem, "Over the Summer Water," is her paean to memory. With its vocabulary (boater, braces, daguerrotypes, esplanade...) distancing its subjects in time, it moves from a jaunty first stanza through the nostalgia of the second, to the *gravitas* of the final lines. There "Water is ghost-freighted with memory," and "widens in rings beyond telling" where, gallantly in the breeze "their scarves and bannerets swelling," "Time's old excursioners go down to sea." These poems offer the pleasure of their harmonies of language, surprises of imagery, and truths of feeling.

Now there is a welcome resurgence among younger poets of interest in formal poetry. The stylistic Balkan wars of recent decades may continue, but poets committed to the shapes of their own talents, as was Elizabeth McFarland, will, as she did, write poems of permanent value.

DANIEL HOFFMAN
SWARTHMORE, PA
APRIL 2007

OVER THE SUMMER WATER

I

THE ACROBATIC HEART

MYSELF

I have stood so long in this place
I have lost account of my face.
I have stared so hard at this tree
I am grown blossomy.

In my branches, words
Bicker like birds.

SELF-PORTRAIT

A mind of revery and neglect,
A sugar-cinnamon intellect;
A sweet in lemonade, stirred to tears,
Made small by mystery and fears.

Her soul was sexless, her heart grew black,
She always wanted her kisses back.
Think of caged lilacs, of ravenous sparrows,
To know why she shot those tender arrows.

THE ACROBATIC HEART

That thin, taut girl, injected by the spring,
Moves in a circus swirl of leaf and song.
The wind's the airy string she dances on
And all her poise is tight umbrellas, swung.

She does not know the wind's become her weather,
But thinks these tilting days with youth will pass.
One might break all his heart and mind together
Imagining some peace for her at last.

Joy gestures in her and she pivots windward,
But soon must fall from tightrope stretch of years,
Her last applause, the vanity of tears
And all her audience in the looking glass.

THE REJECTION

I saw how beautiful your mansions are—
Your lakes and valleys and your peopled plain,
But thought of all that loss with all that gain,
And one geography is not enough.
One world, one world to loose the spirit in,
Will not contain a continental ghost.
I have a dream of islands drunk and lost,
Of cities shining with a ripe decay
Where old ships feed about their harbors' knees,
—Far, far beyond your small and private seas.

VANITY, VANITY

The mirrors of the world don't die.
Behind our glazed and polished sky,
Ghosts of ladies dead and gone
Try lost smiles and graces on;
While bracelets, brooches, hair once bright,
Illuminate our human night.

The little pots of rouge are dust
With Pompeii, Carthage; but the trust
That quickened with cosmetic force
And came from elemental source
Still shines in every blade of grass
That holds the dew for looking glass.

Ladies who touched your eyes with kohl,
Your radiance was of the soul,
And all those tears, that made your fairer,
Live on in your descendant's mirror,
Long since dry age drew you apart
To crack, like glass, your human heart.

EXILES

Everywhere I go I see
Fountains broken quietly.

Eyes that meet mine well through shame:
"Differences" of face or name,
And hands my hands have longed to touch
Were humbled into pride too much.

Dear friend, we ride a train by night,
Beneath a wavering water-light,
Through tunneled grief, derailed despair—
And how then shall I stroke your hair
Or ease your loneliness if your mind
Fears the old cruelties of *my* kind?

From the lost window, prejudice-black,
My own rejected face stares back.

LOST GIRL

Call to her, she will not answer;
Run to her in dreams, there is no embrace.
She has disappeared down an echoing well of laughter,
She has left the place.

All that you know of her was lights and bauble.
As the evergreen glows in a trance awaiting the Birth
Now she holds richest joy and guards hereafter
Her peace on earth.

Look for her, she has changed past knowing.
Ask in the old haunts, there will be no trace,
She has grown into herself, she has lost her girlness
And found her face.

I THOUGHT OF DONNE

I thought of Donne, and how the pride must war—
Of Manley Hopkins, godlier by far,
His filial bemusement death and birth
Counting the spots of God on this, God's earth.

And then, asleep, I dreamed of Henry Ford
Wandering beardless down orchestral ways
Of factories. A patriarchal lord,
Counting his beads of praise.

CLIMBERS

Dusk falls on my roses:
On Purity and Peace,
On Tausenchon and Elegance,
And Pax and Golden Fleece.

I lean from my room inconsolable
To see fair Radiance dimmed.
The shapeliness of roses
No longer clearly limned—

Ah, but their perfume rises,
Now, while the moon smells sweet,
Climb, climb to my window,
Dr. W. Van Fleet!

THE FLOWER

You flower, that greed for rotted ground,
Feed on my thought's warm compost-mound;

Then thought will mould you, flower, to be
Symbol of Beauty's gluttony

That grows not pure, but must infect
Heart and the rubbish intellect

Till, bloated and deformed by those,
You make a poetry of prose,

A garden of a garbage pile,
But chastity of self defile:

Beauty is truth betrayed by the senses,
Written for love and other pretenses.

II

No Other Love

COMMUNICATION

Needing a little more to say
Of what one has
And gives away,
Wanting a trifle less to show
Something your midnights
Surely know,

A poise like flowers in a vase
Arranges my
Disordered face
The while my hand—immoderate bare—
Presses the curvings
Of your chair.

IMAGES

After a time I shall forget
These images important now:
Your eyes, fast darkening, will yet
Live to enlight some other brow.

Your known hand and your mouth will lift
My face upon a foreign hill:
Dream-photos focus, fade, and shift;
Only the heart records them still.

Remembers still, but cannot trace
Who states the negative to "strange":
Love is a dream without a face—
Consistency making prints of change.

BACKGROUNDS

Dear traveling stranger
(Stranger, but more dear—)
Why strangely, known one,
Do you wander here?

Trees have their windows;
Orchards, a wall;
Out of what frame then,
Voice do you call?

I'd draw you to me
With every breath,
Ah, but you knew me
On some lost heath

Or down a wild hillside
We ran our race;
And our loud, ringing laugh sang
The stars out of place!

A LITTLE LIKING

A little liking is a dangerous thing:
Who knows what woes ensuing time may bring
With swift amour? Passion, Romance,
Warm at propinquity as well as chance;
And converse begun mildly, friend to friend,
May leave one lost in longing at the end.
I will not have it thus! Rather deny
Your company than ever cause one sigh
Of want for me when we are far apart
(And I'd not known my throne within your heart).
This risk you take who say you hold me "dear,"
Love me at once—then there's nothing to fear.

His Lashes

His lashes grow like vines upon a string
in tendril mirth, one on another curling
laugh-along lids, a follicle upfurling
as though with fronds he formed a leafy dwelling
for eye-in-awnings is all that he seems

these lashes turn and multiply
and run upon the arms with trellis step
lace up the body in a lattice net
O he could snare the sun in his tight strings
and all that gold pour bursting from her seams

IF I COULD BREATHE

If I could breathe
  Breath into clay
I'd make you turn
  To me and say—

Say what? Are we
  With words concerned?
You need not speak!
  Oh if you turned

That lunar head
  My lost stars wreathe
I'd speak for both
  If I could breathe.

No Other Love

Your gentleness has softened all my days,
When you bend toward me your warm curving mind,
You calm the thoughts that one time coiled and twined;
My name is first of those I hear you praise;
In every room of yours my chair I find—
And you know surer ways of being kind.

Yet still in dreams I see your coin-pure face
Cut out in stone and set where torches hiss,
Washed in the sun, as in a legend's mist,
Borne up by wreaths, high in a flag-filled place,
While I, forgot, shake ravenous for your kiss:
The first is peace. There is no love but this.

PLUMS

We went to gather beach plums while the moon rose
Tremulous, large, impatient from the sea,
Turning our pails to canisters of silver,
Making a fable of the fruit-thick tree.

The sea in glimmering cowl paced back and forth
Chanting a watery "Anguish!" or "Rejoice!"
We had come to gather purple plums by moonlight
And we made our choice.

Sand holds the warmth of sun when day is over;
Rabbitgrass leans to the path the wind went through.
When we left there was moonlight paling over the water
And in our buckets, a plum or two.

Red Is the Green

Red is the green of my delight
A scarlet red, a gold,
Like sunscorched palanquins alight
With lacquer Buddhist-old.

I choose a red that swells the sight,
A red that shakes the heart.
I know its meaning in the night.
We do not sleep apart.

THE TEN-YEARS-IS-A-LONG-TIME LOVE SONG

Dear, if I cease to make
Sweet music for your sake,
The reason you should not break
Your heart:
Song that once rippled throat
With glad, incredulous note,
Joy that once soared (I quote)
"A thing apart,"
Repeated, have become
Softer than heartbeat's drum,
The calm, recurrent hum.
And you, who miss my praise—
O accompanist of my days,
Whatever music plays,
The song's your own!

LOVE'S TOUCH

The hand that knew your youth
When we broke early bread
Will wither out of truth
And falter at our bed.

While words that touched your words
Grow intimately wise,
Thrusting, like timeless birds,
Their wingtips to the skies.

TWO VOICES

HE

When we were young
Old talk pleased best:
Immortality, Fate,
The Will or the State—
And the high-thinking rest.

Now all that's past
And I ponder late
One theme: how young
Are the wild apples hung
High on Time's breast!

SHE

Sir, those long walks
When we two strayed
Deep in the briars
Of Philosophy's glade,
To rest at last
On sweetmoss stone—

Those talks were abstract
For you alone:
My words were curved,
And all my wit
Sprang from your heart
And aimed at it.

III

THE LOST GOLD

THE LOST GOLD

And the lost gold returned—
Heartbreak bright, like the first lost penny of childhood,
Golden as the locket left in a meadow or a lost bracelet
"No child your age should have worn to play!"

Proud and shining as the bronze Latin medal, given to the Friend,
Lost, and the friend lost too.
More gold than gold,
Consoling through its imperfections, seeming to say:
"I am not really gold, nor bronze, nor amber,
But because you love me
I remind you of these and am therefore
Fairer than they."

O bumblebee-colored hair of my little daughter,
O sundrops nestling soft in her neck hollows,
Curls like maple leaves in the Fall when the sun pours through them
Or radiant haystacks holding the warmth of a faraway day,

Your glow is the gold of candles in recollected farmhouses;
Not realistic, now that power has been installed, but always,
My darling, always
Remembered that way!

MOTHER SONG

I sing of all forsaken things:
Torn twigs, rent clouds, disheveled wings;
Brown leaves adrift on autumn's floor,
And letters yellowing in a drawer;
The worm evicted from the rind,
The lamp that in the wind goes blind.

I sing of dreams and treasures lost;
Of all young hope that braves the frost—
Stars locked behind embedded skies,
And little lonely children's cries.
I sing the mother-song of years
To lull the world and dry its tears.

FLOWER MARKET, RITTENHOUSE SQUARE

All dressed in new linen,
The girls of the Square
Are bare-kneed
And fair-kneed
And young as their hair

That shines like shook ribbon—
Like doubloons of gold.
And offers
Rich coffers
Where flowers are sold.

The elderly dear in
The Rittenhouse hat
Turns towards the sun and
Arranges her cat,

While I, under awnings
Wind-bannered and blown,
Barter
A quarter
For blooms of my own.

OFF LITTLE DEER ISLE

A box of sweet grasses
Sun-sucked, meadow-long,
A wreath of young pine cones
Fine candles among;

And the bunchberry redbreast
Atilt those dark leaves
On cold shores where ocean
Sieves, and sieves . . .

O the rowantree lifts there
Rich embroidery wild,
Like a sample of Paradise
By an antique child

Who has opened a box
Made of sweet grass and fern,
And whose scarlet heartberry
Must evermore burn.

FEED MY BIRDS

Feed my birds,
But not the whitethroat in his cage of air!
Feed robin, hawk,
The attendant flock
Of rooftree birds, and birds of prey or prayer;
But not the lost love calling, calling there.

At that wild voice
Trees touch their tips together and rejoice,
Rising full-leaved through waterfalls of sound.
That evergreen lament
Beyond all words has sent
Touch as soft as moss on woodland limbs unbound.

O feed them, scatter seed upon the ground!
Feed homing dove and jay,
Chickadees in black beret,
Feed simple starling, thrush, and small-shawled wren;
But sparrow, the white-throated one,
Feed not again!

PENATES

The hour is late; the Lares blink,
And time is dripping down the sink.
An anxious fire gesticulates
At six familiar, nicked blue plates,
Six knives, six napkins in a row
And six of all the things that go
To make Ourselves. Then feed the cat
And flail the wolf upon the mat.
No force prevails against *these* Fates:
Six knives, six napkins, and six plates.

THE OLD HOUSE

Pictures in the mirror,
Books in the wall
(Imagination's furniture)—
Did anybody call?

Your father called you
Years ago;
Necessity for supper. . .
A dandelion-encrusted lawn
A mower's suburban thunder.

Go to the bathroom and wash those hands!
But tiptoe through the hall;
There's a nettlesome Bee in the sewing room
And the stairs might fall. . .

Or the sky fall down
On the Chicken's head
Or that Old Mother Hubbard
Rise from the shadows
Ghostly wise
Toward an empty cupboard

IV

REMINDERS

ELEGY FOR DONALD MCFARLAND

Forgetting you would be myself forgotten—
Lost in a wave-wash, in the seaweed passes,
Drifting through earth, an anchorage for grasses
With icicles the nails that bolt my tomb.

Forgetting you? Oh, when I have forgotten
It's others' minds must worry to recall
My leaves, *my* grass, *my* seaweed hair and all:
Death shall remember me when I forget you.

POSSESSION

Death has given you to me
In marriage of mortality.
The isolation of your tomb
Is intimate and like a womb
In which I hold you, embryo-curled;
I am your small and private world.
Now only in my love you live
And only breathe what life I give
Since there's no other. I am all
The name now that you'll ever call.
Complete possession! Ah, might it end,
And I be losing you again.

SPEECH

When you and I to death are come,
I shall speak out, who now am dumb.
My unwalled veins, frustrate before,
Into your body's deeps shall pour;
My ashy substance, loosed from flesh,
Will sift beneath your beauty's mesh,
'Til all my strength lies down unfurled
Under the long limbs of the world.

REMINDERS

The day I die
May not dawn fair
But, later, afternoon
Will clear.

A gawky breeze,
Say South-Southwest,
Will hesitantly
Touch your face;

And where you go
To choose my grave,
Flowers will lie
All night for love—

Mosses and stones,
Thin-fingered twigs,
Leaves with the sun
Ablaze in their ribs,

And the soft, incon-
Sequential rain.
And so I'll not
Leave you alone.

OVER THE SUMMER WATER

Summer distances do not alarm
When water fills them;
The eye drinks, feels no harm,
Rinses, and spills them,
While the heart, little red canoe,
Over the resonant river races,
Calling Darling! Clementine! Lou!
O Boy in the boater and braces!

Summer people, like daguerreotypes, don't fade;
They are watermarked, and that is that—
Professor and Mrs. Pew on the Esplanade,
Old Mrs. Ferris's hat. . .
The Fat Boy. . . the Twins. . . the Sophomore. . . the Beaux. . .
The Belles in their bright boating dresses—
Memory wears retrospective clothes,
Slim waists, and (preferably) long tresses.

Summer quivers over the water on a banjo ping,
Is magnified, and roars to shore;
A myriad lost voices in community sing
O my Darling! O Clementine! No more. . .
For water is ghost-freighted with memory;
It widens in rings beyond telling
Where time's old excursioners go down to sea,
Their scarves and their bannerets swelling.